Who Was
Georgia O'Keeffe?

by Sarah Fabiny

illustrated by Dede Putra

Penguin Workshop

For Marc—SF

PENGUIN WORKSHOP
An imprint of Penguin Random House LLC, New York

First published in the United States of America by Penguin Workshop,
an imprint of Penguin Random House LLC, New York, 2022

Text copyright © 2022 by Sarah Fabiny
Illustrations copyright © 2022 by Penguin Random House LLC

PENGUIN is a registered trademark and PENGUIN WORKSHOP is a trademark
of Penguin Books Ltd. WHO HQ & Design is a registered trademark
of Penguin Random House LLC.

Visit us online at penguinrandomhouse.com.

Library of Congress Cataloging-in-Publication Data is available.

Printed in the United States of America

ISBN 9780448483061 (paperback)   10 9 8 7 6 5 4 3 2 1 WOR
ISBN 9780593521397 (library binding)   10 9 8 7 6 5 4 3 2 1 WOR

Contents

Who Was Georgia O'Keeffe?

In February 1951, Georgia O'Keeffe and three friends got in a car and drove from the United States to Mexico. At the time, Georgia was sixty-three years old, but she loved to travel, and a long drive through the beautiful landscapes of Mexico sounded like a fantastic adventure. While she was in Mexico, Georgia would visit her friend Frida Kahlo, the famous Mexican painter. Frida was at home in Mexico City, recovering after a long stay in the hospital.

The two women had met twenty years before, in 1931. At that time, Georgia was forty-four years old and already a world-famous artist. Frida was just twenty-four years old and hoped she might one day become as famous and successful as Georgia. Even though there was a twenty-year age difference between them, the two women struck up a close and lasting friendship. They had a lot in common: Both had quite unique styles of painting, they were each married to men who were powerful in the art world, and they both dressed uniquely to express their individuality.

Throughout their friendship, Frida looked up to Georgia because Georgia was truly one of a kind in the art world. She had blazed a trail in a field dominated by men and had a career that inspired other women artists. Georgia painted what she wanted to paint, dressed the way she wanted to dress, and lived the way she wanted to live—

independently. Georgia had not only inspired Frida, she also had inspired—and continues to inspire—female artists around the world.

CHAPTER 1
Farm Girl

Georgia O'Keeffe was born on November 15, 1887, in Sun Prairie, Wisconsin. Her father was Francis "Frank" O'Keeffe. He was a farmer whose family had immigrated to the United States from Ireland. Georgia's mother was Ida Totto. Her family had come to the United States from Hungary. Ida was a strong, bright woman who had hoped to be a doctor. But when she married Frank, she left school to help with the family farm. Even though Ida had given up her own education, she made sure her daughters as well as her sons were educated. And she taught them to be strong and independent.

Georgia was the first girl born to Frank and Ida and the second child of seven. She had an older brother, a younger brother, and four younger sisters. It was normal for farmers to have large families. They needed lots of hands to help with the farm work.

The O'Keeffes' farm was a dairy farm. They had many cows, but they also grew corn, oats, and hay. Georgia's brothers helped their father with the animals and the crops on the farm.

Georgia and her sisters helped their mother look after the house, cook, clean, and tend to the family's vegetable garden.

Even though there was a lot of work to do on the farm, Georgia's mother made sure that Georgia and her siblings had the opportunity to learn. Mrs. O'Keeffe read to her children all the time. She read them adventure stories and tales about cowboys and the Wild West. Georgia was fascinated. She imagined what it might be like to live out on the prairies and deserts in the western United States.

Georgia's mother not only wanted her daughters to get an education, she also wanted them to have the chance to work and have a career. She hoped Georgia and her sisters would have opportunities to be more than just farmers' wives. So when Georgia was eleven years old, her mother signed up Georgia and two of her sisters to take art lessons. Georgia loved the classes and showed a talent for both drawing and painting.

Georgia spent a lot of time on her own on the farm. The two-hundred-acre property gave her a chance for privacy and solitude. Later in her life, Georgia would say, "I don't take easily to being with people." The trees, animals, and wide-open sky kept her company. Georgia would take her pencil and sketch pad with her and draw the things she saw—raindrops, flowers in the field, leaves on the trees, birds in the sky, and animals in the pastures. The shapes and patterns of these things stood out to her. Georgia tried hard to capture them on paper.

In 1901, just before she was fourteen, Georgia was sent to a Catholic boarding school outside Madison, Wisconsin. Madison was about thirteen miles away from the O'Keeffe farm. The school was just for girls, and it was run by nuns. The rules at the school were strict, but Georgia didn't mind. She studied hard and won awards in several classes, including a gold pin for drawing. On Sundays at the school, the girls had to dress entirely in black. Most of them didn't like having to wear plain, all-black clothing. But Georgia felt comfortable dressed so simply. It was a look that she used for much of the rest of her life.

The next year, Georgia and her older brother, Francis, were sent to a big public high school in Milwaukee, Wisconsin, where they lived with their aunt Lola. In high school, Georgia wasn't really interested in many of her classes—except her art classes. One day her art teacher brought a flower called a jack-in-the-pulpit into class. The teacher pointed out the strange shapes and the different shades of color on the flower. Georgia had seen a jack-in-the-pulpit before, but it was the first time she thought of really looking at it closely and studying its unique features. While Georgia didn't think much of the art teacher, she

Jack-in-the-pulpit

later said, "She started me looking at things—looking very carefully at details."

During the winter of the year she was in Milwaukee, Georgia's parents announced they were moving to Virginia. Some of Georgia's uncles had died of tuberculosis, a disease that affects the lungs. Georgia's father was worried that the cold winters in Wisconsin might mean he, too, would come down with the illness. So in the fall of 1902, the O'Keeffes sold their dairy farm and headed to Williamsburg, Virginia. Georgia and most of her siblings joined their parents in early summer of 1903, at the end of their school terms.

Once they were settled in Virginia, Georgia's parents enrolled her at Chatham Episcopal Institute, a school for girls. Strict rules were enforced at the school, and Georgia and her classmates were there to learn how to be polite and well-mannered young women. But Georgia wanted more than that, and she rebelled against the school's harsh rules. She often got into trouble, and her classmates loved her mischief making.

Chatham Episcopal Institute

During her two years at Chatham, Georgia focused mostly on her art classes. She was so talented that the art teacher, Elizabeth Mae Willis, gave Georgia her own table in the studio. She even gave her permission to work there by herself in the evenings. On graduation day in June 1905, the other girls talked about going to dances, finding husbands, and getting married. Georgia announced, "I am going to live a different life from the rest of you girls." She didn't want to settle down and do what was expected of her. Georgia was prepared to do whatever it took to become an artist.

CHAPTER 2
Art School

Determined to start living her dream of becoming an artist, Georgia moved to Chicago after graduating from Chatham in 1905. There she enrolled at the School of the Art Institute of Chicago, one of the best art colleges in the country. Georgia was only seventeen years old.

Art Institute of Chicago

More and more young women were entering college at this time. But it was still unusual for a young woman to go to art school. Especially when the students were expected to draw nude models.

But Georgia's mother completely supported her daughter's decision, and her teacher at Chatham, Mrs. Willis, had encouraged Georgia to pursue her dream.

At the Art Institute, Georgia learned basic art skills. The classes were based on traditional courses that were taught in Europe at that time. The students often copied plaster casts of antique statues. They followed instructions on how to properly compose a painting based on geometric shapes and principles.

Georgia found some of her classes a bit boring. However, she did like the class taught by John Vanderpoel on how to draw the human figure. Vanderpoel often drew as he lectured the students. He would make big, bold strokes with black and white crayons on large sheets of tan paper. Later in life, Georgia said that John Vanderpoel was "one of

John Vanderpoel

the few real teachers I have known." By the end of her first year at the Art Institute, Georgia was ranked first in her class of twenty-nine women.

Georgia went home to Williamsburg for the summer. During that time, she came down with typhoid fever, a serious disease that causes high fever, headaches, stomach pain, and weakness. Georgia was ill all summer, and her long hair fell out because of the high fever she had. When September came and it was time to go back to school, Georgia was still not well enough

to return. She spent that winter getting better and painting as much as she could.

By the spring of 1907, Georgia had recovered. She thought that she might teach instead of returning to school. But she knew that if she really wanted to be an artist, she should continue her studies. However, instead of returning to the Art Institute, she applied to the Art Students League in New York City. It was where Elizabeth Mae Willis, her teacher at Chatham, had gone to school. Maybe Georgia could follow in her footsteps.

In September 1907, Georgia boarded a train and traveled to New York City. She had experienced life in Milwaukee and Chicago, but New York City was different. It was much busier, more crowded, and more exciting than the cities in the Midwest.

Georgia was thrilled to be in New York City, and she enjoyed her classes at the Art Students

League. She and her classmates painted a lot of portraits and still lifes. (A still life is a drawing or painting of something—like a vase or an apple—that cannot move.) One of America's most famous artists at the time, William Merritt Chase, taught at the Art Students League. He was a very showy man and dressed to draw attention to himself. He taught the students how to use strong, contrasting colors and bold brush strokes as they painted. It was unlike anything Georgia had ever done before. She loved her classes with William Merritt Chase.

William Merritt Chase

Although Georgia was a dedicated student, she was still mischievous. She often ate the fruit that had been used for the still-life compositions.

The Art Students League

The Art Students League was founded in New York City in 1875. It was started by a group of artists who were interested in learning how to paint and draw in a different way. Many of them were women. These artists no longer wanted to follow how art was being taught in European art schools. They wanted to express their own ideas. Instead of having classrooms, the Art Students League was a collection of studios. Each studio was run by a teacher or instructor.

The Art Students League still exists today, and it is run by artists for artists. It is still a collection of studios, and no degrees or diplomas are awarded. Some of the world's most famous artists, including Winslow Homer, Norman Rockwell, and Louise Nevelson, have been students, teachers, and lecturers at the Art Students League.

And sometimes she brought in street musicians and got her classmates to dance in the studios.

One day during the winter, one of Georgia's classmates suggested they visit an art gallery downtown. The name of the gallery was "291,"

and the current show was drawings by a famous French artist named Auguste Rodin. The gallery was owned by Alfred Stieglitz. Georgia was not impressed by Rodin's drawings. And she wasn't impressed by Alfred Stieglitz, either, who argued with some of the students. Little did Georgia know that that trip to 291 would change the course of her life.

At the end of the school year, Georgia won a top prize for one of her still-life paintings. It was titled *Dead Rabbit with Copper Pot*. She also

won a scholarship to study at Amitola, the Art
Students League summer school on Lake George
in upstate New York. It was the first time she
would paint outside of the studio.

When Georgia returned home to Virginia
after her time at Amitola, she discovered that
her parents were having financial troubles. There

was no way they could pay for her to go back to the Art Students League in the fall. Georgia was upset and sad to give up her dream of becoming an artist, but she understood her family's situation. So in 1908, just before her twenty-first birthday, Georgia put away her brushes and paints and moved to Chicago, where she got a job as a commercial artist.

CHAPTER 3
Teaching and Texas

Georgia worked for advertising agencies as a freelance illustrator. At the Art Students League, William Merritt Chase had taught Georgia how to paint and draw quickly. Being able to work fast meant that she was able to meet the tight deadlines at the agencies. Because of that, she was given plenty of work. She drew everything from pictures of lace and embroidery to company logos. One of her pieces, the little Dutch girl symbol of Old Dutch Cleanser, is still sometimes used today.

By being a freelance illustrator, Georgia knew that she could make a lot of money. But she did not enjoy being so busy and working so hard. And this wasn't the kind of artwork she wanted to create. When Georgia came down with the measles in 1910, she decided to go back to her family's home in Virginia. The measles had weakened her eyesight, and she would no longer be able to create the detailed illustrations the advertising agencies needed.

Georgia was sad and frustrated, and she declared that she would give up painting forever.

When she told this to a friend from the Art Students League, he replied, "You are and always will be an artist."

In many ways, Georgia had been an independent young woman. She had gone off to school in large cities and traveled on her own. However, she didn't feel that she had been independent in the way she wanted to be as an artist: She hadn't yet found her own style of expressing herself.

In the spring of 1911, Elizabeth Mae Willis wrote Georgia a letter. Mrs. Willis was going to take a six-week leave from Chatham, and she asked Georgia if she would teach her classes for her. Even though she had said she would never paint again, Georgia was happy to instruct others how to paint and agreed to take the job. She enjoyed being responsible for Mrs. Willis's classes. Her students found Georgia to be a talented teacher who was kind and patient. And she was very interested in

their work. Georgia thought perhaps teaching art was what she was meant to do.

Georgia's younger sisters Ida and Anita were taking art classes at the University of Virginia in Charlottesville at the time. One of the classes was

Alon Bement

taught by a man named Alon Bement. Ida wrote Georgia and told her that he had a unique way of teaching painting to his students. Ida said Georgia should come see for herself.

Alon Bement used the methods of an artist and teacher named Arthur Wesley Dow. Dow's methods of teaching were almost the opposite of William Merritt Chase's. He thought all forms should be simplified and that space should be filled in a beautiful way. Many art schools still taught students to imitate or copy existing works of art. They believed artwork should always be connected to the past. But Dow encouraged his students to look to nature for inspiration and to not worry about artwork that already existed. Dow, and Bement, wanted their students' art to express their own feelings and for students to show more of themselves in their work.

Arthur Wesley Dow (1857–1922)

Arthur Wesley Dow was an American painter, printmaker, and photographer. Born in Ipswich, Massachusetts, Dow studied in Paris. After he returned to the United States to teach, he became a well-known arts educator.

Dow had studied Japanese prints, and he believed that art should be created using the elements of line, *notan* (a Japanese word for the balance of light and dark), and color. In 1899, Dow published a book titled *Composition: A Series of Exercises in Art Structure for the Use of Students and Teachers*. It explained his method and style of painting, and it became a popular book at many art schools in the United States. Dow and his approach to painting played an important role in shaping modern American art.

After she left Chatham, Georgia decided to enroll in one of Bement's advanced drawing classes. Almost immediately, her desire to create returned. Bement's ideas about art taught Georgia that a picture did not have to represent anything in the real world; it could be based on imagination. She realized that "art could be a thing of your own." She felt she now had a way to go forward with a vision for herself and her artwork.

Alon Bement recognized Georgia's talent and asked her to be his teaching assistant for the next school term. But to do this, Georgia needed more teaching experience. She wrote to a friend in Amarillo, Texas, who might be able to help her. Georgia's friend told her that there was a position open in Amarillo: drawing supervisor for the public schools.

At the age of twenty-five, Georgia once again headed off on another adventure. She was excited

about going to Texas. It made her think of the tales of the Wild West her mother had read to her as a young girl. And once she got there, Georgia was captivated by the wide-open spaces and the size of the sky.

Georgia was now responsible for supervising drawing and penmanship for hundreds of students in six schools. She also occasionally gave art lessons. Georgia's students admired their teacher's enthusiasm and love for painting. Sometimes Georgia took her students out into

the prairie. She passed on Dow's and Bement's ways of thinking about art. She told her students that anything could be the subject of their work.

While the students liked the things Georgia taught them, the school authorities were not pleased with her methods of teaching. They wanted her to teach children to draw and paint the way she had learned so long ago, based on what paintings and sculpture had always looked like. But Georgia refused.

In the summer of 1913, Georgia went back to Charlottesville to work with Alon Bement. She started painting again. One of the paintings she did during this time was called *Tent Door at Night*. Georgia used the method that Chase had taught her—painting quickly. But the style was based on Dow's method—composing a picture with basic forms and shapes. The painting shows two large, dark, curved triangles, like the flaps of a tent seen from the inside. The other triangles represent the tent floor and the sky outside. The tent pole cuts the space into even more triangles. *Tent Door at Night* shows how Georgia was learning to express herself and to find her own way of using the new ideas she had learned.

43

Alon Bement thought Georgia would make a good teacher, and he recommended that she get a teaching degree in New York City. Georgia was excited when her aunt gave her enough money to pay for one year of classes. In the fall of 1914, Georgia enrolled at the School of Practical Arts of Teachers College at Columbia University. Another life-changing adventure was about to begin.

Teachers College, Columbia University

CHAPTER 4
Stieglitz and a Show

Anita Pollitzer, whom Georgia had met while they were both students at the Art Students League, was also studying at Teachers College. Anita and Georgia became good friends. They explored the city together and visited as many art galleries and museums as possible. The art world had changed since Georgia had last lived in New York City. In 1913, a big exhibition at the Armory had taken place. It had challenged traditional ideas about what art should be and what it could look like. New ideas about art were everywhere, and Georgia was excited to be a part of it.

Georgia and Anita often visited Alfred Stieglitz's 291 gallery. Alfred was showing works

The 1913 exhibition at the Armory, New York City

that were unlike anything Georgia had ever seen, including paintings by Pablo Picasso. His work showed many views of an object or a person at once. Later, Georgia said, "I didn't understand some of the things he showed, but it was a new wave, I knew that. It showed you how you could make up your mind about what to paint."

Georgia's final grades at Teachers College were not very good, but she did manage to pass the course. Alon Bement wasn't worried about Georgia's grades. He recognized that she had great talent as an artist. That summer, Georgia went back to Virginia to work with him again.

Life in New York City had inspired her. During the summer, Georgia drew and painted as much as she could.

In the fall, she had to make a decision: Should she go back to New York City and look for a job? Or should she accept an offer to teach at Columbia College in South Carolina?

Georgia decided to accept the offer from Columbia College. She would only have to teach four classes a week. That would leave her a lot of time to paint and draw.

But Georgia was not happy in South Carolina. No one wanted to talk about art and new ideas. To keep up her spirits, Georgia would take long walks, paint, and draw. One day, she hung all her drawings and paintings on the walls of her room. As she looked at them, she realized she had yet to find her own style. She had learned a lot from her teachers, but her work reflected them and not herself. She later said, "I have things in my head that are not like what anyone has taught me— shapes and ideas."

Georgia decided to start all over again. She put away her brushes, paints, and paintings, and she began drawing with charcoal on large sheets of paper. Her drawings with charcoal focused on shapes, lines, and sweeping movements. She was excited about them. Georgia usually never showed her work to anyone. But at the end of the year, she rolled up some of her drawings, put them in a cardboard tube, and mailed them to Anita Pollitzer. She asked Anita not to show them to anyone.

But when Anita saw what Georgia had created, she knew she had to share them. Anita took the drawings to 291 and showed them to Alfred Stieglitz. He was astounded. The drawings were new and different, and nobody else was creating art that looked anything like it. Right then and there, Alfred declared that he would put Georgia's drawings in a show.

In May 1916, Alfred hung Georgia's charcoal drawings on the walls of his gallery alongside the work of two other artists. He did not tell Georgia. When she found out, Georgia was angry with Anita and with Alfred. She demanded that Alfred take down her work. But he refused. He told Georgia that some people loved her drawings, and some people hated her drawings,

but everyone in the art world was talking about them. And he wanted everyone to see Georgia's new way of expressing shapes and forms. Georgia realized that Alfred actually understood the style of her drawings and what she wanted to express in them. She agreed to let her drawings stay on the walls at 291.

Alfred Stieglitz (1864–1946)

Alfred Stieglitz was one of the most important photographers of his time. Although he had been born in the United States, his family moved to Germany when he was seventeen. While studying in Berlin to be a mechanical engineer, he discovered that his real passion was photography. He was especially interested in pictorial photography, a style of photography that makes a photo look like a painting.

Alfred returned to the United States in 1890 and was frustrated that art critics refused to accept photography as a form of art. He believed that photographs should be in museums alongside paintings and sculpture, and he spent much of the rest of his life working to make that happen.

Alfred also opened art galleries, where he organized the first exhibitions in the United States of work by modern artists including Pablo Picasso and Henri Matisse. In addition, he was one of the first people to support American modern artists such as Georgia O'Keeffe.

Alfred's photographs were the first to be accepted as works of art by major museums in Boston, New York City, and Washington, DC.

Soon after showing her charcoal drawings at 291, Georgia received a phone call with news that her mother had died of tuberculosis. For some time after that, Georgia was too sad to draw or paint. She had loved her mother very much, and it was her mother who had encouraged her to study art. But by the end of June, Georgia was feeling happier. She accepted a teaching position for the summer at the University of Virginia. She continued with her charcoal drawings, and she began painting with only black watercolor.

After a while, she felt she was ready to go back to painting with colors.

At the end of the summer, once again Georgia was on the move. She had accepted a teaching position in the art department at West Texas State Normal College in the small town of Canyon, Texas. Georgia took long walks through the canyons and across the prairies. There were no fences, trees, or paved roads to break up the view. The fields stretched out in front of her. And the sunrises and sunsets were full of colors and energy.

West Texas State Normal College

Georgia wanted to capture how the landscape and the colors made her feel excited and calm at the same time.

Many people didn't understand Georgia's work. She showed one of her pieces of a canyon to her landlady, who said it didn't look like a canyon to her. Georgia replied that it was a painting of how she *felt* about the canyon.

Georgia's landlady replied that Georgia must have had a stomachache when she painted it!

But Alfred understood Georgia and her artwork. He knew that how her work looked and the moods it captured were special and exciting. In April 1917, Alfred offered Georgia her first solo art show. He included many of the paintings she had done while in Texas. Georgia sold her first artwork from that show. She described it as "a black shape with smoke above it, a picture of the early morning train roaring in." Now she knew that she really could be an artist and that Alfred could help her achieve that goal.

CHAPTER 5
Joining Forces

Georgia taught at West Texas State Normal College for three semesters. During that time, she and Alfred wrote letters and shared their artwork with each other. Georgia felt that Alfred understood her. He believed Georgia had found a "new language" for art.

In January 1918, Georgia came down with the flu. A flu epidemic was sweeping the country, and many people were dying from the illness. Soon

Georgia was too sick to attend her classes. She asked the college if she could take a break from teaching. Alfred was worried about Georgia and her health. He wanted to make sure that she was being looked after. Alfred did not like to travel, so he sent his friend Paul Strand to Texas to bring Georgia back to New York City.

Georgia didn't want to give up her independence, but she knew that being looked after in New York City would be best for her. When she arrived there, Alfred moved her into his niece's apartment, and he visited her every day.

The Spanish Flu Pandemic

The Spanish flu pandemic of 1918 was one of the deadliest pandemics in history. (A pandemic is an outbreak of a disease that spreads to many people around the world.) The disease killed between 20 to 50 million people worldwide. One of the reasons it was so deadly and could spread so quickly was because the pandemic occurred before people knew that influenza was caused by a virus and how to prevent it from spreading. Vaccines had not yet been developed to guard against the flu.

The pandemic struck just before the end of World War I, and many soldiers who became ill with the flu carried it back home with them when they returned from the war. To keep peoples' spirits up during the war, many governments didn't report honestly on cases of the illness in their countries.

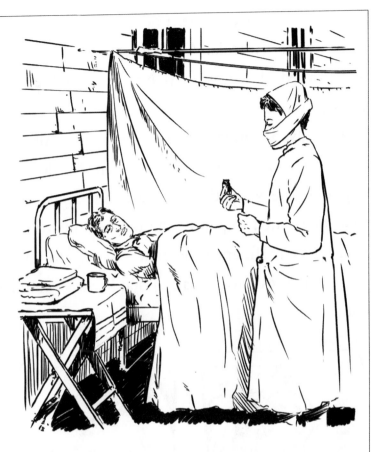

However, Spain, which was not involved in World War I, reported the real number of cases. This created the impression that Spain was hit especially hard by the disease, which resulted in it getting the nickname "the Spanish flu."

Alfred was married at the time, but he had fallen in love with Georgia. And Georgia was in love with Alfred. He was fifty-four years old, and Georgia was thirty.

By July, Georgia was healthy again. Alfred asked what she would choose if she could do anything she wanted for a year. She told him that she wanted to paint. Alfred asked one of his supporters to finance Georgia—to pay for her living expenses—for a year, so that her wish could come true.

Alfred's family owned a summer house in upstate New York on Lake George. Alfred and Georgia traveled there for the summer. Georgia loved the hustle and bustle of New York City. But being outdoors had always been important to her, and she was happy to spend time swimming, rowing, and walking at Lake George.

Soon after Georgia and Alfred returned to New York City, Georgia received two pieces of bad news: Her father had died in an accident. And her brother had returned from World War I, but he was very sick. The news made Georgia sad, but her new life with Alfred helped her get through her sadness. The couple loved and respected each other, and they had settled into a life that suited them.

Georgia's brother returns from war

There were usually a lot of people at the Stieglitzes' house at Lake George during the summer—up to twenty around the dinner table every night. Georgia loved Alfred, but she wanted some peace and quiet away from his family and their guests. She asked Alfred if she could use a shed on the property as her studio. Here, she had the privacy and solitude she wanted. And the landscape surrounding Lake George gave Georgia inspiration for her paintings.

CHAPTER 6
A Focus on Flowers

Throughout the 1920s, Georgia and Alfred continued to split their time between New York City and Lake George. Georgia had painted detailed images of fruit and leaves while at Lake George, but she now started doing close-up paintings of flowers.

She focused on the petals of the flowers, which filled the entire canvas. And the canvases that Georgia painted were large—some over three feet tall. She said, "I realized that were I to paint the same flowers so small, no one would look at them. . . . So I thought I'll make them big like the huge buildings going up." Georgia later wrote,

"I will make even busy New Yorkers take time to see what I see of flowers." In creating these large images of small flowers, she celebrated nature as a strong and powerful force.

In 1924, Alfred's wife finally granted him a divorce. So on December 11, 1924, he and Georgia were married. At the time, a woman usually took her husband's last name. But Georgia kept her own name. She was thirty-seven years old and had already made a name for herself as an artist. She did not want to lose her identity or her independence.

In 1925, Georgia and Alfred moved into the Shelton Hotel. At the time, it was one of the tallest buildings in New York City. Georgia continued to paint images of nature, but she also painted scenes of the city. The energy and power of the city fascinated her as much as the power of nature did. She painted a series of views of the city skyline.

The Shelton Hotel

To capture the changing color and light of the sky, Georgia worked on her paintings during different times of the day. She also painted pictures of the skyscrapers going up in the city. She usually painted them while looking upward from the ground. From this angle, she captured the height and the bulkiness of the buildings.

One of the paintings she did during this time is called *Radiator Building—Night, New York*. The skyscraper rises up in the middle of the canvas. It is hard to see the outline of the building, but the lights from the windows define its shape. It is a very dramatic and almost mysterious painting. On the left side of the painting is Alfred Stieglitz's name in red. The red neon sign that was on the building usually flashed the words *Scientific American*, the name of a magazine. By putting her husband's name there instead, Georgia was openly expressing her love for Alfred for the whole world to see.

Georgia's reputation was growing in the art world. In 1926, Alfred organized a solo show of her work. Georgia insisted that Alfred include her painting *New York Street with Moon*.

Alfred had refused to include this painting in a group show the previous year, and had displayed her paintings of flowers instead.

On the first day of Georgia's solo show, *New York Street with Moon* sold for $1,200, which was a lot of money in those days and about

$18,000 today. Georgia was thrilled and Alfred was impressed.

Although Georgia's cityscapes were most familiar to people, she continued to paint enormous flowers. She wanted to perfect her style of capturing nature close-up. Poppies, larkspur, roses, and petunias became her subjects.

In February 1926, Anita Pollitzer invited Georgia to speak at a dinner for the National Women's Party. Anita had become an officer in the party, which was fighting for women's rights, such as equal pay and protection against discrimination in the workplace. Georgia spoke to the five hundred guests, urging women to develop their own abilities and earn their own living—something that Georgia was beginning to do herself.

Georgia and Alfred were becoming well known around New York City, and when they went out, they almost always wore black clothing. It

was as if they were presenting themselves as works of art. Alfred liked to wear a dramatic black cape, and his white hair looked a bit wild. Georgia often wore a white silk blouse under a simple, black wool coat that was buttoned up to her chin. Her sleek black hair was usually pulled back in a tight bun. Alfred liked the attention he received from the way he dressed. But Georgia wanted her simple black clothes to make her less noticeable and also to let people know she wanted to be taken seriously.

CHAPTER 7
New Inspiration

By the spring of 1928, Georgia felt that there wasn't anything more for her to discover at Lake George. She wanted to find new things to paint. She decided to head back to Wisconsin and visit

her sister Catherine and her aunts. The visit brought back happy memories of growing up on the farm, and she was inspired to create several paintings of red barns while she was there.

Georgia returned to Lake George in August, and she and Alfred settled into their summer routine. But just a few weeks later, Alfred had a heart attack. Georgia put down her paintbrushes and dedicated her time to looking after him.

As usual, when winter arrived, Georgia and Alfred moved back to New York City. Georgia's friend Dorothy Brett introduced Georgia and Alfred to Mabel Dodge Luhan and Mabel's husband, Tony, a member of the Pueblo Nation.

Tony Lujan and Mabel Dodge Luhan

Dorothy, Mabel, and Tony all lived in Taos (say: t-OW-z), New Mexico, and they invited Georgia and Alfred to come and visit them there.

Georgia was excited about traveling back to the Southwest, but Alfred didn't want to join her. Alfred hated being apart from Georgia, but he knew she really wanted to make this trip to the American desert. So in the spring of 1929, Georgia packed up her paints, paintbrushes, and canvases, and set out for New Mexico. Taos is a small town on a mesa with an elevation of seven thousand feet. A mesa (say: MAY-sa) is a hill with a flat top and steep sides. When Georgia arrived there, she felt like she was home. She was overwhelmed by the wide-open landscape, the big blue sky, the intense light, and the extraordinary colors. She said, "It makes me feel like flying."

A building in Taos Pueblo, New Mexico

Georgia spent her days exploring the surrounding hills on foot and on horseback. She visited nearby Pueblo communities and camped in the wilderness. She learned to drive and bought a car so that she could explore more of the area.

One of the first paintings Georgia did when she arrived in New Mexico was called *The Lawrence Tree*. (It was of a pine tree in the courtyard of a Taos home owned by D. H. Lawrence, a famous British author.) Georgia loved lying under the tree at night and looking up at the sky through the branches. And that's how she painted the tree. She wanted people who were looking at the painting to feel that they, too, were lying underneath the tree and looking up at the starry sky. The bottom of the tree trunk looks much larger than it actually is, and the top of the trunk looks quite small. This technique is called foreshortening. By using this method, Georgia was able to express the power and majesty of the tree.

In August, Georgia said goodbye to New
Mexico and headed back to New York. She and
Alfred were happy to see each other, and they
spent the rest of the summer and the fall in
Lake George. When they returned to New York
City in November, the mood was gloomy. The
stock market had crashed in October, and the
United States had been plunged into the Great
Depression. Many people were out of work,

and businesses were failing. Georgia's paintings, however, continued to sell, and Alfred started planning a gallery show of her work.

In February 1930, Georgia's solo exhibit opened. Many of the paintings were from her time in New Mexico. Critics and the public were astounded. They had never seen paintings that showed objects very close-up or cropped the way Georgia had painted them. Many museums bought paintings from Georgia's show.

In April, Georgia headed up to Maine for a week to paint. On her return to New York City, she received an invitation from Mabel to spend another summer in Taos. Georgia was torn about going. She wanted to be back in the desert, but it was going to be hard to leave Alfred. The couple decided that for Georgia to continue growing as an artist, she needed to head back to New Mexico. Georgia said, "I must go for the summer months if I am to continue to live and to paint."

CHAPTER 8
Life in the Desert

During the summer of 1930, Georgia spent most of her time sketching and painting the desert landscape around her. Sometimes she would walk for miles. Other times she would drive her car to a spot, unbolt and swivel around the driver's seat, sit in the back, and prop her canvas on the front seat that was now facing her.

On her trips into the desert, Georgia often came upon sun-bleached animal skeletons. Instead of seeing them as just bones, Georgia saw them as beautiful shapes. She called them her "treasures," and she took them back to her cottage. By the end of the summer, she had a large collection of animal bones and skulls. Georgia carefully packed them in a wooden barrel and shipped it to Lake George. The bones were a symbol of the desert that served as a reminder of New Mexico when she couldn't be there.

In the summer of 1931, Georgia once again traveled to New Mexico. When she returned to Lake George, she began a new series of paintings. They showed a single enlarged skull, sometimes with a flower or a feather, against a plain-colored background or against a desert landscape. To Georgia's surprise, Alfred liked these new "weird" paintings, including *Cow's Skull with Calico Roses.*

But many people didn't know how to interpret them. They thought maybe Georgia was obsessed with death. (After all, these were the bones of dead animals.)

While Georgia insisted that these paintings

were meant to portray life in the desert, perhaps she was expressing some dark feelings. Alfred had developed a close relationship with a young woman who worked at the gallery. This made Georgia sad, but she still loved Alfred very much and didn't want to end their marriage. At the last minute, she decided to stay in Lake George for the rest of the summer and not return to New Mexico.

But Georgia couldn't stay away from New Mexico forever, and for the next couple of years, she divided her time between there and New York. It was a very creative and productive time for her. When she arrived in New Mexico in the summer of 1936, she stayed at Ghost Ranch in a house called Rancho de los Burros. It was a small, U-shaped adobe bungalow surrounded by a patio. The bedroom window looked out over a dramatic landscape. "As soon as I saw it, I knew I must have it," Georgia said.

Georgia bought the house in 1940, and the mountain landscape that she saw from her window became her favorite scene to paint. The flat-topped mesa was called the Cerro Pedernal, and Georgia painted many different versions of it, at different times of year and at different times of day. Each year it became harder and harder for Georgia to pack up her things, leave Ghost Ranch, and return to New York. But she knew she needed to go back and spend time with Alfred, who was now almost eighty years old.

During World War II, it was difficult to live at Ghost Ranch since there was no phone and little electricity. Plus, gasoline was rationed at that time, and Georgia had to drive almost forty miles to buy supplies. So, she started thinking about buying a house closer to a town. In a little town called Abiquiú (say: a-buh-kyoo), Georgia found the perfect home. There were two buildings: one housed her studio, bedroom, and bathroom; the other contained the kitchen, living room, dining room, and another bedroom.

Soon after Georgia bought the house, the Museum of Modern Art (MoMA) in New York City asked her if they could hold an exhibition of her entire life's work—everything from her early paintings and drawings to her most recent pieces.

At age fifty-eight, she became the first woman artist ever chosen to have a major show at this world-famous museum.

Georgia went back to New York City for the opening in May 1946. The show was packed with people excited to view her work, and it received marvelous reviews. After having gone through some dark times, Georgia was happy with her life and her work. But her world came crashing down when Alfred died just two months later.

CHAPTER 9
A Whole New World

In his will, Alfred had said that Georgia would inherit everything he had. That included 850 paintings, drawings, and pieces of sculpture, as well as hundreds of photographs and around fifty thousand letters. It took Georgia almost three years to go through all the items, catalog them, and distribute some of the artwork to museums.

In 1948, Georgia finally found time to start painting again. And in 1949, she moved to New Mexico permanently. She spent the winter and spring at her house in Abiquiú and the summer and fall at Ghost Ranch. After spending years traveling back and forth from New York to New Mexico and feeling torn between two places, Georgia was finally able to call just one place home.

Georgia continued to paint, but she also decided she wanted to see more of the world. She made trips to Europe, Central and South

America, East Asia, North Africa, the Caribbean, Southeast Asia, and the Middle East. Georgia rarely painted pictures of the places she had traveled. She was more interested in how those places looked from above. Looking at the world from the window of an airplane fascinated Georgia.

The colors, shapes, and patterns of the earth from above looked so different, and this is what she wanted to capture in her paintings, like *From the River—Pale* in 1959. During her travels, she also collected stones, shells, and other "treasures" that she used in her paintings.

In 1968, *LIFE* magazine featured Georgia in a cover story. The title of the story was "Horizons

of a Pioneer," and it not only celebrated Georgia's artwork but also the unique life she had created for herself in New Mexico. The article discussed how strong and adventurous Georgia was. She had become a pioneer by breaking rules throughout her life. Georgia always did what she wanted in her life and in her art.

After the article appeared, Georgia became a bit of a celebrity. Photographers came to take pictures of her, admirers came to her home hoping to see her and meet her, and young female artists regarded her as a role model. She was the subject of a TV documentary, and reproductions of her paintings appeared on greeting cards, posters, and book covers.

Sadly, Georgia began to have problems with her vision in 1968, and just three years later she had lost most of her eyesight, at the age of eighty-four. The world around her became blurry and full of shadows, so she stopped painting. But the loss of her eyesight didn't stop her creativity. She began working with clay and hired a young assistant, named Juan Hamilton. He was a sculptor and potter, and he taught Georgia how to make hand-rolled pots. Juan also encouraged Georgia to paint again, with the help of assistants. At the age of ninety-six, Georgia took her last trip abroad, and she and Juan traveled to Costa Rica.

By 1984, Georgia had become too weak and frail to stay in Abiquiú. She moved to a house in Santa Fe, where she could be near doctors and medical care. On March 6, 1986, Georgia died at the age of ninety-eight. She had asked that her ashes be scattered from the top of the Cerro Pedernal mesa, the place she loved so much. Her home in Abiquiú was made into a national historic landmark, and a museum of her work opened there in 1997. It is the only museum in the United States dedicated to a woman painter.

Georgia had once said, "When I think of death I only regret that I will not be able to see this beautiful country anymore, unless the Indians are right and my spirit will walk here after I'm gone." Georgia O'Keeffe's spirit still walks among us, and it continues to inspire people. She was an artist who was considered to be ahead of her time in the way she lived and in the way she painted.

She was a modern woman who blazed her own trail—and she made sure that trail was clear and wide enough for others to follow.

103

Timeline of Georgia O'Keeffe's Life

1887 — Born in Sun Prairie, Wisconsin

1905 — Studies at the School of the Art Institute of Chicago

1907 — Enrolls at the Art Students League, New York City

1908 — Paints *Dead Rabbit with Copper Pot*

1915 — Starts teaching art in South Carolina

1916 — Paints *Tent Door at Night*

1917 — First solo exhibition at 291 gallery, New York City

1924 — Marries Alfred Stieglitz

1925 — Moves to the Shelton Hotel, New York City

1927 — Paints *Radiator Building—Night, New York*

1929 — Travels to Taos, New Mexico, for the first time and paints *The Lawrence Tree*

1931 — Paints *Cow's Skull with Calico Roses*

1934 — First visit to Ghost Ranch

1941 — Paints *Pedernal*, 1941

1946 — Solo exhibition at the Museum of Modern Art

1949 — Moves to New Mexico

1959 — Paints *From the River—Pale*

1973 — Takes up pottery on suggestion of her assistant, Juan Hamilton

1986 — Dies in Santa Fe, New Mexico, at the age of ninety-eight

Timeline of the World

1889 — The Eiffel Tower opens in Paris, France

1901 — Queen Victoria dies at age eighty-one

1903 — First Crayola crayons are invented by cousins Edwin Binney and C. Harold Smith

1906 — The Great San Francisco Earthquake destroys much of the city

1909 — The National Association for the Advancement of Colored People (NAACP) is formed

1914 — World War I begins in Sarajevo, Bosnia

1918 — World War I ends

— Spanish flu pandemic spreads around the world

1924 — The first Macy's Thanksgiving Day Parade is held in New York City

1937 — Pablo Picasso paints *Guernica*

1941 — Japan bombs US naval base in Pearl Harbor, Hawaii, and the United States enters World War II

1955 — The arrest of Rosa Parks sparks the Montgomery bus boycott in Montgomery, Alabama

1979 — Margaret Thatcher elected first woman prime minister of the United Kingdom

1986 — Nuclear accident at Chernobyl nuclear plant in the Soviet Union

Bibliography

*Books for young readers

"About Georgia O'Keeffe." **Georgia O'Keeffe Museum (website)**.
    Accessed September 7, 2021. https://www.okeeffemuseum.org/
    about-georgia-okeeffe/.

"Georgia O'Keeffe: The Making of the Artist, 1887-1950, and After."
    Library of Congress (website). Accessed September 7, 2021.
    https://www.loc.gov/collections/georgia-okeeffe-and-alfred-
    stieglitz-correspondence/articles-and-essays/georgia-okeefe-
    timeline/?loclr=blogpoe.

"Georgia O'Keeffe Biography." **Biography.com**. Last modified April 19,
    2021. https://www.biography.com/artist/georgia-okeeffe.

Robinson, Roxana. *Georgia O'Keeffe: A Life*. New York:
    Harper & Row, 1989.

*Rodríguez, Rachel. ***Through Georgia's Eyes***. New York: Henry Holt and Company, 2006.

*Rubin, Susan Goldman. ***Wideness & Wonder: The Life and Art of Georgia O'Keeffe***. San Francisco: Chronicle Books, 2010.

*Thomson, Ruth. ***Georgia O'Keeffe***. Artists in Their Times. Danbury, CT: Franklin Watts, 2003.

*Turner, Robyn Montana. ***Georgia O'Keeffe. Portraits of Women Artists for Children***. Boston: Little, Brown and Company, 1991.

*Venezia, Mike. ***Georgia O'Keeffe. Getting to Know the World's Greatest Artists.*** Danbury, CT: Children's Press, 1993.

Where to Find
Georgia O'Keeffe's Paintings

The Art Institute of Chicago, Chicago, Illinois

The Cleveland Museum of Art, Cleveland, Ohio

Georgia O'Keeffe Museum, Santa Fe, New Mexico

The Metropolitan Museum of Art, New York, New York

The Milwaukee Art Museum, Milwaukee, Wisconsin

Museum of Fine Arts, Boston, Massachusetts

Philadelphia Museum of Art, Philadelphia, Pennsylvania

San Francisco Museum of Modern Art, San Francisco, California

Whitney Museum of American Art, New York, New York